PRAISE FOR Sacred Stone, Sacred Wa

M000251925

"In this stunning collection, we are offered pilgrimage in its most generous sense. We are given joy in the familiar and the strange. We are given grief in the dark night of the soul and the potent glare of truth. We are given the vast breadth of centuries and the intimate essence of moments. This is the home ground of the heart, and the wending ways of body and spirit."
– **Regina O'Melveny, author of** *The Book of Madness and Cures*

"*Sacred Stone, Sacred Water* is both striking and stimulating…Reading it now I see that I owe a debt to these Americans who came to discover Ireland but in their own way they have made me look at Ireland through New World eyes…shoulder to shoulder, with ancient eyes and young thoughts commingled."
– **From the Foreword by Gerard Clarke, County Meath, Ireland, Irish Guide & Ecologist**

"A gorgeous book . . . From meeting modern stone diviners, to finding the hag-goddess *Cailleach*, to tromps across wet moss to greet old stones, *Sacred Stone, Sacred Water* is a document of a life-altering journey. It reveals the beautiful mystery of an ancient tradition, and the power of ancestral land in sourcing what's essential now."
– **Sonya Lea, author of** *Wondering Who You Are*

"These writers and artists sought inspiration, spiritual connection and personal enlightenment by choosing to retreat to Ireland. *Sacred Stone, Sacred Water* is proof that they found what they were searching for. This book captures Ireland's haunting beauty and mystical history. The blessing is that they have shared it with us. We are grateful."
– **Sue Booth-Forbes, Director, Anam Cara Writer's and Artist's Retreat, Eyeries, Ireland**

"This deeply soul-filled work is drenched in beauty, longing, memory, and intimacy. The land, the ancient stones and wells are eloquent with the voices of the ancestors who speak their wisdom to those who listen."
– **Patricia Reis, author of** *Motherlines* **and** *Daughters of Saturn*

"Carolyn Brigit Flynn has once again assembled a soulful, heart-full feast to savor. *Sacred Stone, Sacred Water* offers a glimpse into the timeless allure, elemental nature, and enduring enchantment of Ireland's magical landscape. For an armchair traveler, the Irish descendant, or simply a soulful pilgrim this book offers deep, pure nourishment."
– **L.R. Heartsong, author of** *To Kneel and Kiss the Earth*

"Open *Sacred Stone, Sacred Water*. Enter the mystic voices of carved stone, falling feather, awe-filled chamber, shimmering well, hidden missive, and simmering interwoven bloods. The taste long lingers. The reverberations flood. Blessed be those who sing the secret phrases of the rocks and rivers, rising suns, stone jewelry, and gas stations of blessed ancient mother Ireland."
– **Pamela Eakins, author of** *Tarot of the Spirit*

Sacred Stone
Sacred Water

Sacred Stone Sacred Water

Women Writers & Artists Encounter Ireland

edited by Carolyn Brigit Flynn

foreword by Gerard Clarke

designed by Janis O'Driscoll

White Cloud Press
Ashland, Oregon

White Cloud Press books may be purchased for educational, business, or sales promotional use. For information, please write:

Special Market Department
White Cloud Press
PO Box 3400
Ashland, OR 97520
Website: www.whitecloudpress.com

Cover image © Fáilte Ireland photographed by Stefen Schnebelt

Cover design by Constellation Book Services

First edition: 2019

Printed in South Korea

19 18 17 18 19 20 21   10 9 8 7 6 5 4 3 2 1

Library of Congress Cataloging-in-Publication Data

Names: Flynn, Carolyn Brigit, editor.
Title: Sacred stone, sacred water : women writers & artists encounter Ireland
  / edited by Carolyn Brigit Flynn ; designed by Janis O'Driscoll.
Description: First edition. | Ashland : White Cloud Press, 2019.
Identifiers: LCCN 2018061111 | ISBN 9781940468730 (pbk.)
Subjects: LCSH: Ireland--Literary collections. | American literature--21st
  century. | American literature--Women authors. | Ireland--Description and
  travel.
Classification: LCC PS509.I68 S33 2019 | DDC 810.9/32415082--dc23
LC record available at https://lccn.loc.gov/2018061111

With thanks to the land and people of Ireland

for their profound welcome, enduring wisdom and ancient beauty

Thanks to Gerard Clarke, our brilliant Irish guide

Also to Trevor Mitchell for companionship and blessed travel

Mary Madison for storytelling and stone divinations

Sister Phil of *Solas Bhride* for guidance and wisdom

Sue Boothe Forbes of Anam Cara Writers' Retreat for beauty and hospitality

and the staff of Bellinter House for exquisite care and elegance

And to the goddess/saint Brigit, divine feminine patron of Ireland

Contents

FOREWORD
by Gerard Clarke

I have worked as a guide in Ireland for more than 25 years, and it was under that heading that I first met Carolyn Brigit Flynn in 2002. She was bringing a group of writers to Ireland, and needed someone to show them around the Boyne Valley. Thus began a connection that has continued, broadened and deepened over the intervening years. Carolyn, I discovered, was not only a creative writer and poet but a woman who was passionate about her roots and equally passionate about her love of Irish heritage and culture.

She brought a fresh way of looking at what we take for granted here in Ireland and presented it to her fellow American travelers and seekers. I gradually came to understand what was required of me, but also realized that these visitors had a great willingness to explore the way Irish society now lives in a landscape steeped in history, archaeology, folklore and tradition.

I have worked at many of the major historical sites in Ireland, but the times I spent at Newgrange and the Hill of Tara have been some of the happiest years of my life. At Newgrange, I was lucky to meet renowned academics as well as poets, musicians and deeply spiritual people. I was also in charge of the Hill of Tara, Ireland's most sacred ritual site, for five years. The exploration of Tara in every discipline taught me about the influence of landscape, history and beliefs on the creation of a national identity. The challenge as a guide was to put all that into a coherent and logical interpretation for those not of Irish background.

Carolyn and her groups of writers and artists would arrive in Ireland every few years. Each visit brought its own dynamic but also a joyful, passionate and at times irreverent look at Ireland. The works produced by the fourteen dedicated and inspiring artists in *Sacred Stone, Sacred Water* are both striking and stimulating. Looking at the art and photographs and reading the deeply felt poems and prose brings back the excitement and joy that was in the air each day as we progressed from site to site. The wealth of knowledge and experience each brought, their willingness to listen, and their beginning to understand what being truly Irish means is humbling.

Reading it now, I see that I have grown in their company. I owe a debt to these Americans who came to discover Ireland, but who in their own way have made me look at Ireland not just from the traditional viewpoint but through New World eyes. That has impressed me, but also given me the confidence to be proud all over again. That we can stand there, shoulder to shoulder, with ancient eyes and young thoughts commingled.

Working with these groups has not really been work at all; rather a chance to affirm my beliefs in the ancestors, in our landscape and in the people of Ireland. While my role was to be the introducer of Ireland to the group, I was always conscious that their journey onwards after our four or five days together would involve meeting different interpreters in different parts of the country. Carolyn has chosen well with all of her Irish locations and guides.

Sacred Stone, Sacred Water is a thoughtful, warm collection of connections, reactions and statements of a diverse group of people from all over the United States, brought together by their love of art and of Ireland. I look forward with eagerness and anticipation to our next Irish American encounter.

Beir bua dibh, agus beannachtai deithe na cloiche` is na h-uisce oraibh go leir.

Best wishes and the blessings of the gods of the stones and the waters on you all.

–Gerard Clarke
Ecologist and Eco-Spiritual Mentor
Mayo and Meath, Ireland

PREFACE

The predawn autumn equinox morning was dark and crisp as we climbed the hill of Loughcrew, also known for its old Irish name, *Sliabh na Cailleach,* or "Hill of the Old Woman." Our twenty-minute walk had begun in twilight darkness; we could still see stars in the Irish sky. Still, as we climbed we were at the cusp of time. As we crested the hill, the sky was cerulean blue—otherworldly and clear. A few stars still shone.

Before us was the sacred passage mound of Loughcrew, an apparent grassy hill about 30 feet high, lined with huge megalithic stones. Back in the day—that is, 5,000 years ago—this "hill" was a dazzling mound of immense stones covered in small white quartz, with an inner chamber large enough to hold a dozen people. Each year on the autumn and spring equinox, the rising sun—then and still today—precisely enters the inner chamber and illuminates the carved stones within. The ancient symbols carved upon the stones seem to glow and pulse. It is a breathtaking sight.

That is, if the sky is clear and the sun emerges from behind the clouds. Which is never taken for granted in our beloved Ireland. I've climbed Loughcrew on Equinox morning in the past only to be met by low, gray skies. That morning, however, the signs were good. We found our place in line alongside some two hundred other women, men and children. There was a hush as the horizon turned pink, then rosy salmon, too bright for words, then the orange sun peaked the hill and touched our faces. It is not exaggeration to say that every single human on the hill that morning was beautiful. Our much-loved guide, Gerard Clarke, and our wonderful driver, Trevor Mitchell, had climbed the hill with us. All of us wore the wide-open face of awe.

In this book, you will see that the solar alignment occurred, and we were there to witness it. You will read the poetry and writing that unfolded, and see photographic images of an unrepeatable moment. You will, as well, enter countless other moments—small encounters and epic sights—that occurred during our two-week journey. Our time in Ireland seared each of us and changed us thoroughly. To share what we saw and felt, we used poetry, story, essay. We used the lens of our cameras and the click of our phones. We used pen and ink, paintbrush and lithograph.

What emerged in *Sacred Stone, Sacred Water* is a vision of Ireland not often seen. Most of our group of fourteen women writers and artists have photographs in this book, but I want to acknowledge Janis O'Driscoll and Suzanne Daub, whose photos grace many of these pages. As I watched the two of them with their cameras, holding still for the shot, I understood that we had seriously good art in the making. In particular, I want to offer gratitude to Janis O'Driscoll, whose design for this book elevates these works into a single, elegant vision.

Our journey was a writing retreat, and we wrote every day. As we journeyed, I was deeply moved by each woman's writing and poetry, which seemed to spring from a unique collaboration between her individual spirit and the ancient Irish landscape. The group included published writers, artists, novelists, poets, photographers, painters, medical doctors, healers, musicians, educators, political organizers, social workers, and international women's activists. The work of this talented circle was elevated, intelligent, soulful, and finely honed. Ireland had opened all of our hearts, and we took up her invitation.

Ours was an intimate journey, and *Sacred Stone, Sacred Water* is an intimate book. Everywhere we turned in the Irish landscape, stones had outlasted millennia and water was all around, often falling from the sky. Our group of writers and artists let all of this enter. With this book, you can join us.

–Carolyn Brigit Flynn

INTRODUCTION
Three Beautiful Parts of Ireland

Sacred Stone, Sacred Water emerged from a writing retreat and tour in three remarkable parts of Ireland, focused upon mythic places and sacred sites that still live prominently in the Irish landscape. Our journey included the **Boyne Valley**, about an hour north of Dublin in the east, the **Beara Peninsula** in the scenic southwest, and the ancient town of **Kildare** in the midlands.

This book is organized thematically rather than by geographic area, and in this section I will tell you a bit about the places we visited and the images in this book. As you read *Sacred Stone, Sacred Water*, if you are taken by a particular photograph, you can find the name of the photographer as well as the location indexed in the back.

For readers who have been to Ireland, the images from these three wonderful parts of the island will bring her magic to you all over again. If you have not yet been, the writing, images and art will give your heart and spirit a new journey of its own. Perhaps *Sacred Stone, Sacred Water* will inspire you to travel to *Éire* yourself, or to return. You will always be grateful for the chance to walk the land of this wonderful new/old world.

Boyne Valley

We began in the verdant Boyne Valley, which is famous throughout the world as the location of Ireland's premier ancient site, the majestic passage mound Newgrange. Ever since my first visit to Newgrange in 1996, I have remained thunderstruck by a love of the old sacred stones of Ireland.

Newgrange is a remarkable feat of engineering and astronomical knowledge, and archeologists conclude it is most appropriately called a monument or a cathedral. It was built 5,000 years ago of megalithic stones, each about eight feet tall and weighing about two tons. The indigenous Irish placed these massive slabs of granite laying sideways in a huge circle about the size of an acre, and then built a passageway of vertical standing stones about sixty feet long into the circle. At the end of that long entrance, they built a stunning inner chamber of stones, all carved with intricate designs, including Newgrange's famous triple spiral. Following a form developed over several centuries, they covered the chamber with layers of stone and soil, to create a huge mound about 40 feet high and 250 feet across.

The construction of Newgrange 5,000 years ago, without motorized power of any kind, is amazing enough to dazzle the modern mind. A thousand years older than Stonehenge in England and the pyramids in Egypt, it is one of the oldest extant buildings in the world. Inside, Newgrange is intact, dry, profoundly quiet and church-like. The great mound endured in Irish myth and folktale through the ages, and was known as *Bru na Boinne,* or "Mansion on the River Boyne." But the most remarkable aspect of Newgrange was re-discovered in the 1960s, when archeologists found that the inner chamber was precisely designed to receive the rays of the rising sun on the Winter Solstice. To walk through the passageway of Newgrange, to experience a recreation of the rising Winter Solstice sun as a pinhole of golden light broadening to fill the inner chamber, is to touch an enduring aspect of the human spirit.

Our group spent a day at *Bru na Boinne,* along with its nearby sister mound Knowth, which is equally large and stunning with two openings, one oriented to the Equinox sunrise and another to the sunset. We visited a small passage mound on the Hill of Tara, with its own solar orientation to the cross-quarter days of *Imbolc* and *Samhein* in early November and February. And on one incredible dawn morning, we climbed the sacred hill of Loughcrew and experienced the sunrise Equinox alignment directly ourselves.

The Boyne Valley has been continuously occupied by humans for 9,000 years, and all of this settlement occurred around the valley's central organizing element: the River Boyne. This beautiful, slow-moving ancient river is older than the last Ice Age. Her earliest known name is *River Bóuvinda— Bó* meaning cow, a sacred animal in Neolithic Ireland, and *vin* meaning white or illuminated. Thus the Boyne was anciently known as the "River of the White Cow Goddess."

This great river was always nearby as we explored the many ritual places of the Boyne Valley. We visited Ireland's ancient monastic sites from the 5th to the 15th centuries: Kells, Monasterboice, Bective Abbey, with their bucolic stone ruins and magnificent Celtic crosses, intricately carved with biblical motifs and stories. These places, and the ancient towns that grew among them, make the Boyne Valley a profound place to fall in love with the Irish landscape, and to touch many eras in Ireland's long, remarkable story.

Beara Peninsula

From the Boyne Valley we journeyed to the Beara Peninsula in the southwest, a somewhat off-the-beaten-path part of Ireland, full of marvelous, hidden gems. Or not so hidden, as we came to see as we arrived, wide-eyed as we all were with glorious views of the sea, the cliffs, the shoreline and the lakes and rivers of the Caha Mountains.

Surrounded at all times by the sea, our group stayed in lodges above the ocean, near the ancient port town of Castletownbere. All around us were remnants of old Ireland, a world of water and of stone, the last vestiges of old Irish churches, stone circles, and venerable standing stone circles. We spent a day at the Anam Cara Writer's Retreat in Eyeries, and several pieces in the book were written there, where we could settle in, write, and enjoy the fabulous cascading waterfalls of its grounds. Sue Boothe Forbes of Anam Cara introduced us to the Irish storyteller and stone diviner Mary Madison, who unforgettably offered us her deep insight and lyrical stories, giving us old Ireland in a pure, unfettered form.

But it was our day exploring the Ring of Beara and its ancient landscape that most changed and grounded us. The rain poured in buckets all day long. Still, we told our guide that yes, we wanted to hike in boots and umbrellas across three drenched, muddy fields to the Ardgroom Stone Circle. Built 4,000 years ago, the stones stand together in a kind of eternity, withstanding human hazards and the endless wind and rain. As the Irish skies poured, we felt what we might have missed on a sunny day: that the stones are alive, they have personalities, that they too suffer and absorb the elements of life. They have stood as silent witness to humanity for four millennia, from the time of the very ancient Irish who set them there, to us modern-day women in our rubber shoes and engineered waterproof coats.

That same day of endless rain, we drove to the Hag of Beara, one of southwest Ireland's iconic spirits. She is a craggy stone on a tall cliff at the edge of the sea, and in folktales is known as the earthbound remnant of Ireland's old woman of the land, The Hag of Beara, or the *Cailleach*—the same old hag woman of Loughcrew. The stone Hag of Beara was laden with offerings: coins, flowers, jewelry, beads, clooties or prayer cloths, all faded and worn by sun, wind and rain, and now part of the ancient divine woman in her stone version. We knelt before her in the pouring rain, and one of us wept in her presence.

The port town of Castletownbere was a constant delight during our time in Beara. We enjoyed an evening of traditional music at MacCarthy's Pub, explored the old Irish town of longtime taverns and modern mobile phone stores, fishing gear and upscale cafes. We sighed once again at how wonderfully Ireland mixes the ancient and the modern as we sipped excellent Irish tea, strong coffee, and of course, a pint of Guinness or a glass of Irish whiskey, or two.

Kildare

The divine feminine of Ireland remained with us as we journeyed to the ancient town of Kildare, where we immersed ourselves in the spirit and tradition of Brigit, Ireland's famous goddess and saint. We began with a visit to Brigit's Holy Well, where we blessed ourselves and each other with her healing waters. We kneeled and prayed, and left our offerings and intentions on the sacred tree above the well.

Among the great gifts in Kildare today is the opportunity to visit the Catholic sisters of *Solas Bhride* Centre, the name meaning "Brigid's Flame" in Irish. In 1995, the sisters re-lit Kildare's eternal flame to Brigit, which, incredibly, was once tended ritually by priestesses and nuns for at least 800 years and perhaps much longer in the mists of time. The sisters and their community now carry Brigit's flame and spirit forward, honoring both the goddess who was a patroness of poets, holy wells and the eternal flame, and the famous saint who traveled with her people into the Christian era as protector of the poor and downtrodden, mistress of the land and animals, builder of monasteries and the educator of women.

At the site of Brigit's monastery in Kildare, we visited the Fire Temple where her eternal flame burned. We explored the massive round tower of what had been her thriving medieval monastic center and walked the grounds of her abbey. We spent a day of writing and retreat at the newly built *Solas Bhride* Centre, an acclaimed, modern center for Celtic spirituality devoted to Ireland's indigenous ways of caring for the feminine spirit, the earth, and each other.

Later in Kildare, we had the good luck to happen upon excellent traditional music in a pub, dancing with the locals and raising a pint or two. Afterwards the musicians, charming, older, witty men, took out their phones and made sure we all became friends on Facebook. This and other moments brought us into modern-day Ireland and her people, who everywhere met us with calm grace, humor, intelligence, and dignity.

I come from this land, as my grandparents were born here. I visit often to renew my connection with the ancient landscape and to see my Irish cousins, who keep me grounded in the world of modern Ireland. Still, one of the great joys of my life is to bring others to this beautiful Old World landscape. Our group of writers and artists, many with their own Irish heritage, formed a living tapestry as we traveled in September 2016. To have created a book by such talented people, with writing and art inspired by such beautiful parts of Ireland, provides sustenance that goes deep. These pages bring me joy; may they feed your soul. May they offer praise to the ancient spirits of old Ireland, *Érie*, who live on, still.

–Carolyn Brigit Flynn

WELCOME

This

This land wide open
The scent of tundra on its mossy body
Skin torn and healed into
Massive rock slabs—
This land calls me home.

Heather, lichen and herbs are
in its welcome bouquet.
Crouched bushes tell
Of the wintery gale.

They invite me into homes
They hold in their midst.
Merry small buildings
Huddled together to tell
Stories of long gone inhabitants.

They murmur in a language
Only history knows
Accented by a robin's call
Beginning with a fluty song
And finishing with a shiver
Evoking a sweet melancholy
And a sense of
Soothing solitude.

– Ursi Barshi

8

She Calls

When day is done, and the clatter
and cacophony of the world's roar subsides,
I hear her.

Gentle lapping waves along the Aran Island shores,
echo of surf crashing 300-foot cliff fortress walls.
The crunch of gravel under hiking boots
headed for solitary mountain trails.
Lone hikers tuned to the melodies of sheep and wind,
the generous quiet of green rolling hills.
The blazing music of fiddles and whistles,
bouzoukis and bodhrans spilling from pub doorways
into the rain-washed streets at midnight.
Hearth fires still being lit from peat
gathered in backyard bogs. The very particular shade
of softened golden light falling between
rainbows and rain.

Megalithic passage tombs sharing secrets
with those who listen. Stone circles waiting
to add their quiet strength and silent messages.
The music of an ancient language, sliding sideways
into the Irish tongue. Sheep and wild shades of green
that meet your eyes in every direction.
Wisdom of old ways.

Ireland has called again. She has become a siren song.
Traveling across the waters. Whispering through
the California pines and old growth redwoods.
Blowing across dry parched grasses
of my drought-stricken state.
Coming through my window.

Landing on my pillow.
Entering my dreams and my waking.
Finding me, once again, across time and distance.
Like a lake, stream, river, sea,
Ireland is Friend. Lover. Teacher.
Hearth. And Sanctuary.

Though I thought she did not know me,
though my name was from another land,
Ireland called to me across the waters
and landing on her shores
I had come home.

–Sarojani Rohan

Fáilte. Fáilte. Fáilte.

You are welcome here.
May this moment usher in a new era,
where I embody the light of the Universe
and stars coming through me,
where I am the crescent moon
put up over the gate to the festival.*

–Judy Tsafrir

**Inspired by a poem "When I See You and How You Are"
by 13th-century poet Rumi*

What Brought Me to Ireland

Ireland actually brought *me*. It sought me out and gently but unrelentingly marched me through the necessary steps. Each part of the journey here was prepared by a "deeper river than I am," to use a phrase borrowed from Jenny Comeau.

The sudden longing for this land was born of desire that began long ago, without my realizing. My father told me of his trip here twenty years ago. He could not stop talking about his encounter with a group of schoolgirls... the joy he felt experiencing their energy and beauty. Somehow, he caught how different they seemed from the ones he might have known back in the States. I remember feeling curious. What really touched him so deeply, eclipsing every other memory of his experience here? Was he just feeling so different because of the land, or was it simply the adventure of travelling to a foreign place that was exhilarating for him? Was that really the beginning of my longing for the place?

I now find myself at a strange and unfamiliar juncture. After retirement, basic logistics and a new lifestyle are established. This opens and frees me up to truly begin my golden years, my third act, my fourth quarter. Oh! I so wish them to be hearty and rich and deep! That inevitable Blue Bus will come calling to whisk my spirit away. How to make best use of my time here and now?

Know Thyself rings true in my ears—in my head—and joins the tinnitus already present. Tinnitus. A constant reminder that my head is already reverberating with sensations of the afterlife. So please, prepare me for more unknown! May I be ever more familiar with the inner landscape, to help ground and heal and experience more of the Joy I deeply know is there waiting for me. Salud!

–Jessica Webb

14

Field After Field

Field after field after field of come-alive green, separated by rows of melancholy green. Fields running up hills on either side of the road. In the distance, dots of jewel-toned sheep grow and grow until I recognize them by name.

My beloved cows far outnumber the people I see. I am thankful for that. There are communities of deep black, spotted black and white, and several tones of brown. Always they seem peaceful, no matter the sun, the pounding rain, the grazing on a steep incline. They recline and eat and nuzzle as if this is the best day of their life. I wish I spoke cow to eavesdrop on their dreams.

This Irish landscape of field after field after field opens up my own nooks and crannies, where I can air out some of my old stories, that are so welcomed by these fields of fifty shades of green.

–Sandy Dempsey

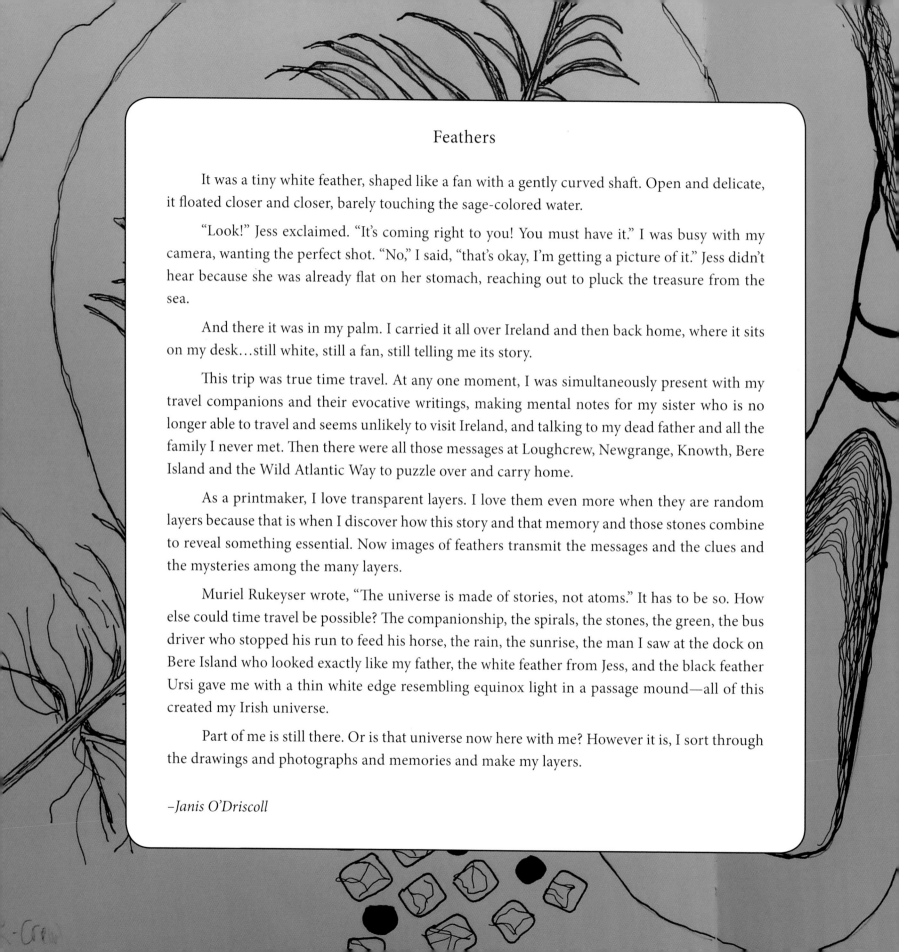

Feathers

It was a tiny white feather, shaped like a fan with a gently curved shaft. Open and delicate, it floated closer and closer, barely touching the sage-colored water.

"Look!" Jess exclaimed. "It's coming right to you! You must have it." I was busy with my camera, wanting the perfect shot. "No," I said, "that's okay, I'm getting a picture of it." Jess didn't hear because she was already flat on her stomach, reaching out to pluck the treasure from the sea.

And there it was in my palm. I carried it all over Ireland and then back home, where it sits on my desk…still white, still a fan, still telling me its story.

This trip was true time travel. At any one moment, I was simultaneously present with my travel companions and their evocative writings, making mental notes for my sister who is no longer able to travel and seems unlikely to visit Ireland, and talking to my dead father and all the family I never met. Then there were all those messages at Loughcrew, Newgrange, Knowth, Bere Island and the Wild Atlantic Way to puzzle over and carry home.

As a printmaker, I love transparent layers. I love them even more when they are random layers because that is when I discover how this story and that memory and those stones combine to reveal something essential. Now images of feathers transmit the messages and the clues and the mysteries among the many layers.

Muriel Rukeyser wrote, "The universe is made of stories, not atoms." It has to be so. How else could time travel be possible? The companionship, the spirals, the stones, the green, the bus driver who stopped his run to feed his horse, the rain, the sunrise, the man I saw at the dock on Bere Island who looked exactly like my father, the white feather from Jess, and the black feather Ursi gave me with a thin white edge resembling equinox light in a passage mound—all of this created my Irish universe.

Part of me is still there. Or is that universe now here with me? However it is, I sort through the drawings and photographs and memories and make my layers.

–Janis O'Driscoll

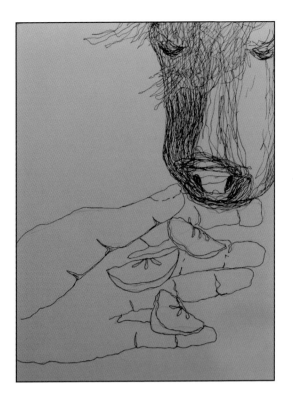

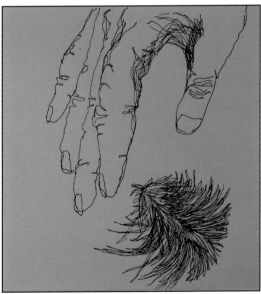

Feather Drawings & Relief Print by Janis O'Driscoll

"Red Feathers"
–Janis O'Driscoll
Lino print, 14.25" x 12.25", 2016

Scribe

Perhaps this journal will be the silent beginning to a new invitation into writing, slowly, purposefully, by hand. Imagine the days when to write required a feather pen, appropriately sharpened, ink from berries and minerals, and vellum made by hand from the skin of sheep. By the time the writer sat down to write, sacred implements had been prepared and the die was cast: what was set down had import, was rare, rarified and secret in its very being.

May this journal be such a place. The pen was handed to me pre-made, and the paper bound by someone else. But may these words be benediction, true to what is difficult, braided, wounded and strong. May these words be faithful to all that is—the great worlds that live outside me and within me, the holy presence, the secret vow, the One.

–Carolyn Brigit Flynn

The Grass Sings

The grass sings under the weight
  of yesterday's Irish rain,
grey skies poured an elixir of green
   onto our afternoon and evening.

This morning the sun rose golden,
   unfurling a bright, blue sky.
Long blades of green grass offered up notes of glory
   braided with birdsong.

My heart opens to this new day.

Breathing in, I inhale molecules of my first family,
   my grandparents' very same air
I see their heartaches, their glory, their wisdom
   I glance down at my hands.

All of our hands reflect the light in this dawn.

–Jean Mahoney

LIGHT

Autumnal Equinox

For five thousand years people have climbed
this mountain,
hopeful for the sun's rays to bless their journey
into the dark cycle of the year.
We are among the latest of those
as we begin our way up in the 5 A.M. chill.
Early morning mist rises, so thick we think
we see rivers
all over the landscape.
Some of us recognize the fairy's welcome.

I look at the faces around me,
and see rooks and rivers,
vast horizons and the thousand griefs
we have all sustained.
The cycles of the moons and tides,
the prayers of the angels. Each face—a holy place
emblazoned this equinox morning
with golden light from a Sun who has
seen us fit to receive the light.
Through no particular merit
of our own, just a grace extended
to the needy, the hungry, the wounded, the seeking.
Yes. A sunrise like none other
in the history of the world.
Pilgrims. Beggars. Revelers. Bent and broken.
Jubilant and the immortally youthful.

Oh those greens! Those infinite shades
of Ireland. Brigit's green mantle
spread in every direction.
Some in jubilation beat drums
and drink fire water from Tibetan singing bowls.
Others stand quietly in wonder,
grateful that they have made it up the mountain.

We take our turn, leaving the long line
as we stumble over the threshold stone,
through the passageway, in a small circle
joined in holy union,
hearing each other's heartbeat
in that chamber of a passage tomb,
made 5,000 years ago.

And it *is* illuminated. And we do see
the ancient carvings on the back wall
as we slip through time, between worlds.
Now we are the ancestors,
and the stone carvers and the mound builders
and the barefooted devotion of the faithful.

We become the lit torches,
and the singing and the revelry.
The messages of old are shared and seen
as we huddle together in the ancient stone
chamber, remembering we are all
children of the Great Mother.

True to the promise of any sacred opening
the chamber expands and suddenly
there is room for all, as a pheasant flies in,
followed by a dog.

The stars have all aligned
and are looking down at us
pleased we chose right this morning
to not go back to sleep, to climb the mountain
in predawn darkness
to face the wind and chill of this high place
to gather both in hopeful expectancy
and in surrender to what would be.

The Divine, then as now,
shape-shifts from Goddess
to Guru to Female High King
to Holy Mountain
to Sacred River to Wagging Tail of Happy Dog.

How can I not be on my knees in gratitude?
For these legs that carried me up the mountain?
For I know, too, that someday
I will not be able to make this journey.
Yes. This blessed moment in the freshest air
on the very first morning of the world,
praising the light with the sheep and the dogs,

the drumming and the shofar, and with my tribe
names known and unknown.

Did I "see the light"?
Dear God and all things holy
Yes! I saw it in that glory be morning—
and also in the bus driver
who deliberately stopped to share an apple
with a horse on the side of the road.
This holiness. Oh my. Not "Where is it"?
But, can my little heart take it all,
because I hear in the wind
that it is everywhere.

–Sarojani Rohan

25

Autumn Equinox at *Sliabh na Cailleach*

Sandy was the first of our group to emerge from the passage mound, bowing down under the low stone doorway, face glowing, lit by the sun rising in an almost cloudless sky. Illuminated, like the intricately carved stone at the back of the mound's inner chamber—which lies in shadow except two hours at sunrise a few days a year, when light and dark balance.

Sixteen of us hiked slowly up the steep hill through sheep pasture in near dark, some leaning on aluminum poles in place of ancient wooden staffs. We carried offerings of stones, tobacco, cedar. Hearts beating fast, we sought an opening, Earth's womb, creation's mystery.

One by one we passed through the gate, then circled the mound step by step sunwise. In dim light, we glimpsed lichen-covered kerbstones of the mound, then faced east toward a slice of lightening sky. Below, low spots in the undulating green landscape filled with white mist, like the shallows of a great sea. Mist, too, is a doorway, a threshold; in the mist shapes shift, reveal magic.

As the orange arc of sun rose above eastern hills, the sound of drums, ram's horn, pennywhistle and rattles reverberated against stone, vibrating our bones. Strains of the Great Song entered the mound, the body of the goddess, fierce grandmother *An Cailleach*, for whom this hill is named. The first slanted rays of the sun reached in and brushed the inner stone's green velvet, painting it gold.

To see the light we each had to block it for a moment, clamber over the high stone threshold, duck under the lintel, feel our way into darkness, crouch like women in labor, huddle together like twins or triplets swimming in the womb's inward sea—then settle, gaze at the sun's rays on the stone as if no one had ever seen it before.

No one had. Not one of us had ever been the person we were in that moment, seeing that light on that stone in that way. We each became someone new, the one who emerged from the passage, the birth canal, the doorway between life and death, light and dark, certainty and mystery.

Our newborn faces glowed in the dawn. We were held in every cell, every step, by the grandmother.

–June BlueSpruce

30

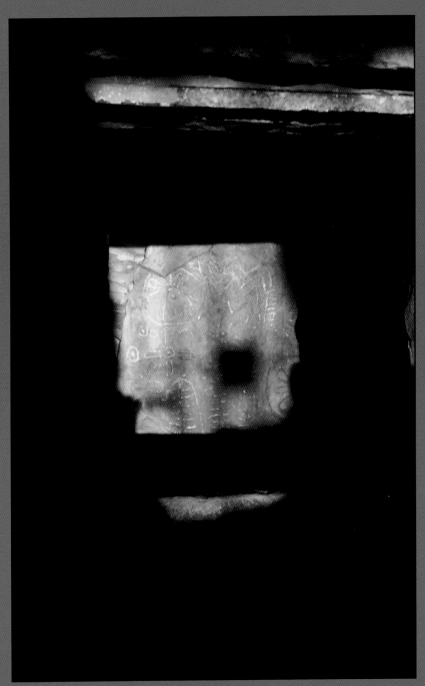

The Other

She stood on the hill. Both of us gazed eastward, anticipating the growing dawn that would bring the Fall equinox sun to shine upon us and the sacred stones, set deep within the earth passage mound of Loughcrew. Her hair was tangled blond, tucked into a red knit cap. Without words yet, we watched the rolling fog streaming through the far hills below, the tips of which were slow motion whitecaps, as like the ocean.

This beauty made us instant friends and lovers. I turned and asked her name. "Catherine," she said. With a "C" or a "K?" I asked. With a "C", she replied.

"My name is Jess," I said.

We embraced. We looked deeply into each other's eyes. "I love you, Catherine," I said with soft intensity. "I love you, too," she said.

Then, drawn again back to the brightening majesty of the dawn, we faced the red fireball which illuminated the sky, the fog, and our faces.

Two women, one old, one young, meeting in this brief moment in time, drawn together to reach across the chasm of "the Other" to join in intimate celebration and trust.

–Jessica Webb

Sacred Jolt
Sliabh na Cailleach

I wanted to taste the carvings with my tongue, let their textured shapes tell their story into my mouth. I knew I would never find the words to describe it, no matter how earnest my pen or my heart.

An Irish friend told me, "You will find the words. You will find them."

And so my mind returns to the seconds after I emerged like a newborn into the light. I remember thinking, "Holy moment." Holy, the pre-Christian word that comes from Old English meaning, "to make whole."

Holy, a word that comes from ancient Gaelic for holly, a sacred tree of the ancestors.

I remember hearing, "Rest is for sissies," as if The Hag rasped into my ears alone.

The sacred jolt of a moment inside the womb of the Great Mother has birthed something restless in me –a profound ecstasy. Ecstasy without the gaudy sparkles that ecstasy usually gives off. No, a deeper, transcendent feeling.

This one knowing I know: with each and every new sunrise that my eyes witness, I will again be shepherded into the fierce and awe-filled chamber of that holy moment. And each time, I will not find the words. The taste will linger in my mouth. The song will carry on the winds.

–Jennifer Comeau

After Loughcrew

It feels that the light has entered me. I close my eyes and see it. I touch my heart and feel it. Something echoes in the hollow of my chest.

It revolves around light. It revolves around the dance of the spinning planet as we revolve around the sun. It has to do with what it is to capture light. To take the rising light of the sun and to allow it to be channeled at a particular hour on a particular day, into a particular Beauty. Isn't that the essence of writing, poetry, and all art? Something is channeled out of the general Beauty into a specific moment, a specific Beauty.

Now, on this day of all the days of my life, I saw the light. The very light I have thought about, read about, taught about, written about for twenty years.

On this day of all days, I saw the light. It is indeed impossible to describe. So delicate, golden, sweet, inviting. So inviting. I feel invited. I feel invited into life. The message is, After all the striving, there is now rest within being. After all the wishing, there is fulfillment. After all the doing, there are things now done.

There is nothing to try to become. There is only living inside the self, this self, flowing, shifting, changing with the rivers. There is nowhere to go, but everywhere.

–Carolyn Brigit Flynn

On This Morning

Dance with the trees, old hag
go back to the days
before you were young
before there was salt in the sea
before the architect threw down the gauntlet
before your tears turned to shards
of impiety

On this morning the sun rose
for you and you and you
and everyone sang her own beatitudes:

> Blessed be the women who climbed this hill
> Blessed be the mist that welcomed the sun
> Blessed be Diego of Loughcrew who circled
> the mound without wonder—but with delight
> Blessed be the skirted man in green with his
>   tribute horn
> Blessed be our guide, his feet made of Irish soil
> Blessed be all the bare feet who have trod
> this cold green earth that is their home
> Blessed be all that entered the womb of the
> Goddess on this day, 22nd of September, 2016

So dance, old hag,
today you have no age rings
today you have no grieving bones
today the fire of the equinox
flows through your veins
Let the beat of the drums
pulse through you
as the wind pushes the trees
to reveal a holy rhythm
Let the songs of the mounds
lift you—and all of us
to shimmering skies

–Linda Serrato

Dimensions

I wouldn't have made it up the hill in the light. It had to be the early morning darkness that charted the course. The darkness left me breathless as I kept climbing, breathless and focused.

It wasn't until I emerged from the stone cairn that I understood that I was sitting in more than one dimension. Quiet and still inside the cairn, I was really trying to imagine the old ones and young ones who had visited here and said their prayers. What were they feeling? How did they express their gratitude?

As we walked around and visited the other cairns, I was struck that I had just become an old one who had left her energy and gratitude, and I wondered if someday, someone would walk up in the dark, enter into the light, and reflect upon the energy that I left with these stones hundreds of years before.

As I walked down the hill in the light, I asked myself if I had used my time wisely in this sacred place.

–Sandy Dempsey

STONE

Who Will Roll Back the Stone?
(*In Honor of the Newgrange Entrance Stone*)

Who will roll back the Stone? Were we the women going to the tomb? Did you see the angel saying, "He is not here." Risen by the Sun and led into the Light. Empty but Presence everywhere.

Were we the women going to the Tomb? Did you see the markings? The reminders of all that is important in life.

Light—Water—Earth—Air

We asked aloud what was the message being conveyed. In 5,000 years the message has not changed. It is still there.

Light—Water—Earth—Air

Don't make it too complicated! The message hoping that some generation 5,000 years from now will still remember.

Light—Water—Earth—Air

If we honor and care for these, that is all that needs to be.

Were we the women going to the tomb? What did we come to see? Three spirals on a wall. Linked spirals, interconnected—perhaps one for the sky or star-filled heavens; perhaps one for the earth; perhaps one for the otherworld.

We are coming to know the star-filled heavens—the cosmos of black holes, and far off solar systems. We have learned much about the earth. But what do we know of the Otherworld? Where or who are the astronauts and explorers who will take us there? What mysteries await our knowing?

How will we hold in reverence what we learn, so that once more three spirals can dance?

–Anne Fitzgerald

Boyne Valley

Once I was a stone, then I was a bear, now I am a stonemaker, a mosaic artist who is perpetually on the lookout for future art materials. This passage mound seems like the perfect place to grab a few stones. I have monkey mind. Take? Leave? Taking is wrong, I know, but I want some. I could casually put a few small stones in my pocket. Who would miss them?

This is ridiculous. I am in the presence of 5,000-year-old work, a Neolithic age passage tomb monument, and this is what preoccupies me? These stones have witnessed thousands of years of life passing by, supporting whole villages on their backs, waiting patiently for us to arrive and go. They are life absorbers, story keepers, and carriers of the whispers of our ancestors. My grandparent's bones are built of these stones. The earth is not my shopping cart.

I drag my mind back to this moment. A young man, with a smiling and open face, announces to me that this is his mecca, his annual pilgrimage. Last year, he says, he arrived sober. This year, he thought he'd take it in drunk. What about me, he asks, what's my state of mind?

I smile, I breathe; I let the rocks go. I silently witness the enormity of this ancient accomplishment. I reclaim my stonemaker inheritance. What would happen, I wonder, if I opened my heart to the woman who knows that once in ancient starlight, she was a stone?

–*Suzanne Daub*

Teach Yourself to Read Your Stone
For Mary Madison

The white-haired stone diviner tells me, "Teach yourself to read your stone." The stone I had described, just down the old road from my house in Maine, is called *Spirit Rock*. Local lore says indigenous women made medicines on its vast, high tableau.

To my next question, the stone diviner says, "It is not only seeing the stone with your psychic eye, it is just seeing." She adds, "See it each time as though it were the first time, and it will reveal something that is only there at that moment." There and gone like the mystical Brigadoon that emerges from the primordial mists once a century.

"You see," she leans in, eyes cornflower blue with crinkles, the smile of an ancient conspirator, "the stone changes as you change."

I am taken aback. "These beings, old as millennia change as I change?"

"I read my stone, just outside," she waves toward the front of her cottage. "And it is always changing."

I wonder, does a new patch of pale green or carmel yellow lichen just appear one day? Does a different cast of light, like the flaming red of a winter sunset, reveal something in the stone heretofore not seen?

How our minds blind us into seeing the same thing when it doesn't exist. It is not the same river today. It is not the same stone. I am not the same woman.

I made her a promise – to teach myself to read Spirit Rock and the etchings and stories it contains.

I have always felt stones had moods. Now I understand they change. They change. I change. Back in Maine, on the grounds I steward, I melt into Spirit Rock and I am invisible as a man and woman pass me on the road.

–Jennifer Comeau

ANCESTOR

Carrying My Dead

When you died, the light went out and I stayed there with you in the dark. Laying in the stone basin, I curled my body around your ashes. You were waiting, and I was keeping a vigil in the dark space, in the dark stone cave of my grief. No candles here to dispel the place where I knew I could find you always.

But when the first tender light slipped over the lip of the morning, you went with its ebb. You went to where all the others were gathered, and I knew I would have to choose life. And I did. But it is a life that cannot forget the old story, the one I was never told. The one your death brought alive in me.

The story where the dead rattle in the night like the dried oak leaves in October, or the singing of the blue mussel shells at the tide line. There is something there in the dark recesses, among the old stones, a secret language of renewal only the dead speak.

And there is someone there too. In the deep hour of the night when I am frightened, I run my fingers over the spiraled grooves carved there into those stones older than time.

You are there and all the others too, and their stories. Still. I have marked those stones with my blood so that they will know me, know the whorl of my fingertips as I find my way back through the dark to curl around you once again. To rise and to carry your stories into the light.

–Nora Jamieson

To My Mother, One Month Gone

The reality of your absence
becomes clearer with each
passing day and each version
    of the moon at night

The reality of your death
    becomes softer, wider and
    benevolent in ways I could
    not before imagine

Standing at noontime
    underneath the Irish sky,
    clouds billowing, building rain inside
    while all around a brilliant blue
    and green, green, green below my feet
    my hazel Irish eyes see
    in ways I haven't seen in a long while

I imagine you up there
    just looking down at me here
and I see your people—all the ones
    who've been waiting for you
    for many years

I see our clan, glad to be rejoined
    with you, who were the oldest among us,
    now the youngest there

When I went to Newgrange, the stones
    whispered *Peace*
 I breathed the outward breath
    of one who helped birth you
    into that peace,
    the peace you know now

Walking,
walking into the light
You didn't need that four-wheeled walker
    anymore
    No more fear of falling
    No more fear of failing
Now you are welcomed
into freedom and family

When you were alive I used to think
    visiting different places on earth—
    say a remote redwood forest
    or walking by the sea with
    the tide coming in

I used to think, "If my mother could see me now!
What would she think of my adventures?"

Now I am practicing not thinking that anymore
Because I know you can see me
and for this I am glad

"Look at me now, Ma. Look at me."

–*Jean Mahoney*

Father

1. Land

He was 47. I was 25. He came towards me. He was drunk. I stood up and held my fist out to him. I shouted, "If you ever come towards me again, I'll kill you." My mother and brother watched in silence, then my brother escorted my father out of the room.

Yesterday, I could feel his presence. It was the softer side of him. I think he is relieved I have finally come here, so that we can have a conversation. He wants me to know about his roots.

The land has already begun to soften me. Yesterday, I kissed that big old wise beech tree and felt its pulse in mine. The silence here is like his silence. I can feel him trying to give me some gifts. Whether I accept them is another story.

2. Labyrinth

Rain, rain, rain, rain, rain. This is what I feel: the beautiful rain in my bones. This is what I say as I enter the labyrinth: "What is the question?"

I am walking for 10 minutes. It begins to pour. I am so happy. I do walking meditation, in and out, round and round.

Very softly I feel his hand in mine. It is my father. He is younger. I am my 10-year-old self. We walk together, step by step. This time his steps are not bigger than mine. We walk side by side, comfortable, easy, soft…just as it should be.

He breathlessly lets go of my hand. I hardly notice. My tears mix with the rain, seeding the earth with a good memory. This was the first time I have thought about my father without the past interfering since his death 21 years ago.

3. Newgrange

Our guide, Mary, said about the passage mound that there is a time where the light is coming and going and the veil is thin. I feel this and see an image of my father slightly in front of my right shoulder. The image, too, is slightly veiled, but I can see him.

He makes his presence known in a manner that I can take in. I am not afraid that I am seeing him as Spirit, and I am not afraid that I am seeing him at all. This is a different father. Death has revealed his truer self, and he is now revealing that to me. So we have both put down our past for the moment to meet each other as the light passes from one realm to the other.

54

4. Synchronicity

On our last day in Ireland, many of us went shopping. I had found a few things to bring home for friends and family, gifts which represented the beauty and spirit of Ireland—rich, colorful textiles, healing water from St. Brigid's well, and a local artist's rendering of a cow that one of my mates found for me.

I was on my way back to the bus, completely in my skin after such a rich and unforgettable two-week journey, when I happened upon two of my Ireland group. They had found a jeweler who designed and created many unique items. They invited me to come along, as one of them was deciding whether to purchase a piece.

Jess was looking at a beautiful *Ogham* necklace (pronounced o-am), the meaning of which was "Love." Ogham is the oldest known form of written Irish. It is depicted simply as horizontal and vertical lines, each of its twenty letters named after a tree.

I was completely taken with the necklace that Jess was looking to buy. Wanting to give her space to make her decision, I wandered around the store, looking for another Ogham "Love" necklace. Behind a locked glass case, I was drawn to a slightly larger *Ogham* necklace, which appeared to have the same depiction for "Love."

Unknown to me, Jess had made a decision to purchase a different necklace. When she had completed her transaction, I told the owner that I would like to buy the necklace in the glass case, which I assumed meant "Love." He said that he was sorry to disappoint me, but that necklace had a different meaning—"Dad." I felt the hair on my arms rise.

"I'll take it," I said. When I moved to the counter to pay, I saw that Jess had not purchased the Ogham necklace, "Love." I decided to buy both of them.

As the jeweler was wrapping up my two pieces, he told the three of us that the *Ogham* "Dad" necklace was made three months ago for Father's Day, but that no one bought it. It was the only one he made.

I wear the necklaces together. A friend said, "You are wearing 'Dad Love' and 'Love Dad.'" This was my father's parting gift to me.

Whenever things seem intractable or beyond hope, when something appears immovable and unyielding, I am reminded of this journey to Ireland where I found my father again. I had denied him a presence in my life for so long. But in the heartland of his beginning, he reached out to me. We forged a new relationship, one that includes our roots, our history and our future. All is possible.

–*Sandy Dempsey*

"She Who Dwells Here"
–Jessica Webb
Acrylic on canvas, 30" x 40", 2016

Upon arrival, we met an ancient beech tree on the Bellinter House grounds, which many of us called "Grandmother Tree."

Rising up from the deep loam
Of ancient memories
She who dwells here
Remembers.
As modern day well-maidens
We are reawakening and
Are inspired.
The world needs us
To listen
To hear
To rebalance
Ourselves and all humanity.

–Jessica Webb

The Territory of Memory

Recently, in the wake of returning from Ireland, I dreamt these words—

The Constitution does not protect the territory of memory

I had gone to Ireland to walk the land of my ancestors, of my dead. Finding my County Cork kin only recently, in addition to my Northern Ireland ancestors, I wanted to walk where they walked, with the prayer that the land who they had loved, who had loved them, had given birth to them, would speak to me as a daughter. Claim me.

I have been looking to be claimed by clan my whole life. It's an embarrassing admission at sixty-seven, open to accusations of wannabe, and all kinds of psychoanalytic interpretations. But it's true and I'm training myself not to use the psychologized language of obsession to describe this unceasing desire to find the through-line of my people.

I've come to believe that my dead, their memories, their stories are calling to me—that they are longing for me. That somewhere in the ley lines of my soul, they live. They're not perfect, not ideal, but they carry knowledge of the way to live with earth as kin, to pay debt to the Spirits of the land, to live as a full human being.

Chief of the Cherokee Wilma Mankiller once said something like this to her people—if you follow the through line of your people, you will be alright. I have not one bit of Native American blood in my veins, yet her words spoke to me deeply. The through line. The author John Berger writes, *The dead surround the living. The living are the core of the dead. In this core are the dimensions of time and space. What surrounds the core is timelessness.* He goes on to say that before the dehumanization of society by capitalism, the living and dead were interdependent, and that religion used to be concerned with these mystical exchanges. Long before organized religion, reverence for and communication with the ancestors was the spiritual foundation of many old cultures.

The indigenous peoples of North America carry their own diverse cultures, that echo what many of us of European lineage have lost. Rather than co-opt theirs, indigenous Elders encourage we seekers to find our own ancestors' ways. I am charged to remember what I was never told. I am called to remember the stories that I am sure run in my bloodlines. I am called to remember and honor the stories of my dead. Out of these rememberings, I am called to help create a viable earth culture, where species speak to each other, where we learn to become full human beings in relation to each other, the earth, our dead, our ancestors.

So many are doing this. We are apprenticing to the land, to the wind, the water, the stars. We search old texts, read between lines of ancient poetry, follow the wild text of our animal kin through snow and mud, and dream. We use our hands in the old ways of making and working, to uncoil the remembering in our blood and brain. We search for the nearly lost ways, in my case of Gaelic cultures, lost but for the vapor trail of recent Elders now crossing to the Otherworld. And we dream.

The Constitution does not protect the territory of memory

I am a woman woven of four bloods. Is the soul of each blood different? I am of Scots, Irish, English and Scandinavian decent. I am a daughter of Puritans who first immigrated to North America and settled what is now Cape Cod and Massachusetts, and Windsor, Connecticut. Some of my Scots people came in 1718, fleeing Ulster in Northern Ireland, and moving into Maine and Canada. My great-great-grandparents emigrated in 1872 from Northern Ireland to settle in Enfield, Connecticut. My ancestors from County Cork came before the Famine, settling eventually in Machias, Maine, where they established a successful lumber business.

I am a woman woven of four bloods. I am a daughter of Occupiers, whose ancestors occupied Wampanoag, Pequot, Mohawk, Maliseet and other indigenous homelands. Who established homesteads on stolen territory, declaring rights to thousands-of-years-old established hunting and fishing grounds. I am descended from Indian fighters, who fought in the Pequot War and King Philip's Wars, defending their rights to stolen land. I am descended from hard workers and hard fighters. Some of them had been honed razor sharp by a history of persecution by the British, the Vikings and the Romans. They came here and proceeded to do exactly what had been done to them, seemingly without much question and often motivated by terror of what they saw as the American wilderness, and savage. Savage is how the British sometimes described the Irish, distinguishing them from "whiteness" and civilization, which the British laid claim to for themselves.

There is no doubt that those who came to America from other lands, and from whose blood I am descended, suffered. That some of them came to America desperate and fleeing hardship, tyrants and starvation. But this is not the whole story, nor is it the only version I can lay claim to.

As I traveled through Ireland, thousands of North American indigenous peoples had gathered in North Dakota to stop the expansion of the Dakota Access Pipeline under the Missouri River. They called themselves Water Protectors. They understood their actions to stop the pipeline as ceremony. They made a human wall of prayer and dissent, to obstruct the private and public militarized police forces who had come to remove them with dogs, rubber bullets, pepper sprays, and sound cannons. And legislation. They stood in faith with the old ways, the ways they knew were in alliance with mother earth. Water is life. The old laws.

I am a woman of four bloods. The English warred on the Irish and the Scots, the Ulster Scots then occupied the land of the Irish. And then there are the Vikings. As I prepared to travel to Ireland, and then once there, I felt a war between my bloods. The old wars had become interior, now an internal dialogue of longing, prohibitions, rights, and lack of. Where do I have the right to walk, what earth can I claim as kin? Who am I? Where are my people? To what land am I kinned?

In Ireland, I was continually yet subtly reminded of the devastations inflicted on the Irish people by the British and the Ulster Scots who are also my ancestors. Repeatedly, a dawning sense of familiarity with the sacred iconography of passage tombs and standing stones, and with the people who created them, was shrouded with heartache and a responsibility not to deny the whole of my lineage.

Rain pelted, stinging against our faces, our rain gear ballooned and snapped in the wind as we climbed over the green stepladder straddling the fence. We were in the open countryside of County Cork, near the ancient village of Ardgroom. A very large and beautiful cow, her sides perhaps bulging with calf, stood watching as we proceeded up the wet cow pasture. Large cow paddies sat on tufts of green grass, glistening with pooled water, as we stepped carefully around them navigating the boggish ground.

The tall stones sat on the hill. They are there now, under the low sky, arranged in a circle. Immense, silent witnesses to timelessness. On that day, I approached the north stone, and slipped behind it. Taller than the other stones, aligned with the north star, it stands a bit outside the circle. Hidden, I leaned into the rough granite, mossy and licked by cow's tongues, and I wept long-stored tears. I have been remembered. And I have remembered. I rubbed my tears onto this old memory keeper, I licked the rough stone, and I prayed. I wanted to stay forever.

Leaving, I was reminded of my grief as a child at having to leave my father's people after rare visits. My people who I might not see again, and if so, only rarely. My connection to him. I felt I was leaving kin, and I turned as many times as I could to catch a last glimpse of the family of stones.

The Constitution does not protect the territory of memory

Indigenous peoples of the world know what land has been given to them to protect, to call home, a right given by the land itself, by their deep intimacy with that earth, the water, the animals, the plants. The land of Ireland is filled with cairns, passage graves, standing stones, sacred burial grounds, and ceremonial sites acknowledging the Otherworld of the ancestors. Mysterious, inscribed stones speak a language known by the heart and our old memory. Of tectonic forces and old powers of creation, of what and who is sacred to a people.

I am thinking of the people of Standing Rock in North Dakota, who stand for protecting the sacred. They have experienced hundreds of years of devastating oppression and its attendant poverty and despair. And yet, there are the Memory Keepers. They stand now for their old ways. Are they carried by the Standing Rocks, those keepers of earth's memory? Might we all be? The Constitution does not protect the terrain of memory, no.

But neither can it regulate nor legislate memory, because memory in the earth, in the stones of earth, is written in scripts all over the world. Waiting. Perhaps it is they, these abiding keepers of memory who enter our dreams, who speak to us of ancient possibilities and ways. A through line. To home.

–Nora Jamieson

Hunger

After I moved to Seattle in my mid-twenties, after fleeing the farm near Bellingham where I tried and failed to kick Valium cold turkey while breaking up with a woman I loved and sinking into almost suicidal misery, after months of wandering with a flask of rum in my pack wherever I went, after nights with my lover Susie when we would drink a half-gallon of wine between us and I, too drunk to make love, could only cry and Susie would ask me why I felt so punky, after the birthday party for a man I didn't know well to which I brought a fifth of Jim Beam as a gift and then insisted that he open it so I could drink some and we finished the whole bottle, after realizing that, although by this time I was only drinking one beer a day, I really needed that beer, I decided I needed to clean up my act.

All at once I stopped: taking Valium, drinking alcohol, eating meat or any animal products, drinking caffeine, indulging in chocolate or sugar in any form, and having sex (this part was not entirely voluntary). I started following a strict pattern of eating called food combining. I don't remember all the rules, but they restrict which types of food you can eat at the same time. For example: it's OK to eat certain proteins, like nuts, with low-sugar fruits like grapefruit; otherwise eat fruit by itself on an empty stomach. Don't eat animal proteins (meat, poultry, fish, eggs) with starchy foods. Wait a few hours between restricted combinations. Etc.

I once asked a man I knew who lived in a collective household near my apartment on Capitol Hill why my food combining chart said to eat avocados alone. He said, "If you eat avocados with other people you have to share them," and laughed. It had never occurred to me that it was possible to have a sense of humor about this.

All these changes and restrictions threw my digestive system into turmoil; abdominal cramps sometimes kept me from eating much for days at a time. But I stuck with the diet, assuming the pain was a healing crisis I just had to get through. I doubled down, lost thirty pounds, had no discernable fat on my body, and stopped having periods. I regarded my long, bony form with a kind of wonder. Others, especially the women in my improvisational dance group who saw me naked or in leotards, felt growing alarm. One ventured the possibility that I was anorexic. Offended, I denied it.

Finally, even I had had enough and sought help from legendary naturopath Joe Pizzorno, one of the founders of Bastyr College of Naturopathic Medicine (now Bastyr University). Joe spoke English so fast that people thought he was speaking Italian. He advised me like an Italian grandma: "Eat!" His prescription: Forget food combining. Eat lots of carbs. Resume dairy products to replenish my intestinal lactobacilli. "Potatoes! Pasta! Calories!" I rapidly filled out, the digestive problems disappeared, and my periods started again.

Recently, it hit me that when all this took place, I was the exact age at which my Irish-American grandmother Florence died in the flu pandemic of 1918-1919, leaving my mother, age three, and her baby brother motherless. Florence's grandparents, born in County Cork, Ireland, survived *An Gorta Mór*, the Great Famine of 1845-52, during which a million Irish died of starvation and epidemic diseases. In the years during and after the Famine, two million survivors, including some of my ancestors, left Ireland for the US, England, Canada, Australia, anywhere they could get a ship to take them.

I first visited Cork in 2012, searching for information about and a feeling of connection to these ancestors. Information was sparse and elusive, but the connection I yearned for seeped from the stony mountains, ancient oak trees and rugged coast into the cells of my bones, the hum of my blood.

In Ireland, the residue of famine remains. Simple stone plaques in graveyards honor the victims. A sign marks the original site of the *Oispideál An Fhiabhrais*, the Old Fever Hospital in the village of Clonakilty, where people were treated during the virulent epidemics that accompanied the famine. My bed and breakfast host told me stories of the many who died along the roads on the way to the hospitals, too weak to go one more step. The Irish population is still, over a century and a half later, far less numerous than before 1845.

I returned to County Cork to honor my ancestors. To affirm to them that life has been passed on to six generations (so far) since they left. To thank them for giving me life. To release myself from carrying their suffering.

Grandmother Florence, you died so young. Like so many before you. Those who perished in the Great Hunger lost everything. Those who survived and left Ireland lost so much: the land that birthed them and buried their kin; their family, language, sense of belonging.

I don't have to starve on their behalf. Against all odds, life got through to me. I owe it to my ancestors to take it in, dance it, live it.

–June BlueSpruce

O Come All Ye Rovers

(to the tune of Swallowtail Jig)

O come all ye rovers to places so pretty
Take leave of the noise and the cares of the city
To follow the glens and the dales that abide
The call of the lark and the sea as your guide.

(chorus)
The phoenix that soars over Bonny Portmore
The cry of the free that are servants no more
Be brave and be bold knowing your gifts are true
The ancestors' wisdom now singing through you.

Ireland whistles the tune of the Goddess
Tales of the magic and lore of the forests
The famine the exile the battles the rise
Of tigers and homecomings tender and wise.

O Come All Ye Rovers
and gather together
To relish the music, the magic, the weather
Farms, pubs and stone circles, trails by the sea
Welcoming all to the grand mystery.

--Sarojani Rohan

Song Note: Many years ago, on my first journey to Ireland, I encountered and fell in love with the soul of Irish music. It spoke of blood-soaked battlefields and the sorrows of exiles and hardships, ancestral heritage, and the resilience of a people who endured. Soon after, I helped to form a Celtic band, playing the penny whistle.

We have played the traditional Irish instrumental "Swallowtail Jig" for years. One night in a pub in Castletownbere, encouraged by my intrepid writer friends, I sat in with the locals at a music session, and played the instrumental version of Swallowtail Jig. Upon arrival home, I realized that I could finally finish lyrics I had started a few months earlier, after being in Ireland, feet in the soil, offerings made, with music from the pubs still ringing in my ears.

Solas Bhride — St. Brigid in Kildare

Image after image. The circle, the sunlight, the cross being woven. The cross being blessed by each member of the circle. What have we woven here?

Without seam the tradition of the fire being tended by the priestesses of old; the fire being lit and tended by Brigid and her monastery sisters, and now the fire being tended by a trio of Brigidines.

Who will continue to carry the flame? What will they say; what stories will they tell of how the ancestors of the current century carried the flame? Will there be Garden of Eden apple stories of generosity? Will there be weapons of war sold to feed the poor or educate the illiterate? Will there be an earth restored?

What if the ancestors of old could whisper to the future beings what is needed—so we might hear the message of what is needed for these times clearly and loudly in both ears—a blessed surround sound of invitation to compelling action?

–Anne Fitzgerald

WATER

Reflection at Castletownbere

Ships at sunset
their bodies
bobbing with the tide
a tender rocking
like a mother's newborn
lullaby sway
then after dinner
boat lights glimmering
in the dark water
casting a faint glow home

I think of reflection
meaning to think, to muse, to ponder
or   is it
to put a mirror to my soul
my heart

It's been many years
since I've walked
by harbor lights
heard the lapping
of water
against pylons
over rocks and sand
since I've stared

at wrinkled boats
in a bay
smelled the briny scent
of my childhood

Tonight I was taken
to the other side of the world
to my home
& as I walked toward the bus
I closed my eyes
listened hard
for the soothing melodies
of foghorns

–Linda Serrato

Fishing Vessels at Sunset

They stand at attention, waiting to catch the evening sun. Proud and privileged, fresh with paint, lined one after another. They know their duty. To bring fresh catch each week to feed the families of Castletownbere; and to send it on to their inland neighbors. Precise, well rigged, diesel engine—a match for the unpredictable Atlantic seas.

I wonder if they remember their ancestors. The *curraghs*, the wrapped wooden-hulled boat with single sail who listed precariously as a net of fish was lifted over the side. I wonder if the seas or the rocks speak to them of mighty waves that rose unexpectedly as rogues to lift up and smash down these wooden forebears.

I wonder if they say a prayer as the sunlight breaks the mist of morn. Or if they bless themselves when the clouds turn black, and hide everything from view. Or if they sing their gratitude when the sun sinks on the horizon wearing lines of color blended only for this day.

I wonder if they glimpse the widows standing even now on the wharf remembering and still longing for the fishing boats that did not return.

How do they bow or tip their hat in solidarity and recognition? A horn is much too loud; perhaps a single ring of the captain's bell.

Ritual, recognition, remembrance.

–Anne Fitzgerald

Heart Wide Open

I sat in the solarium at Anam Cara, in a spot that felt like being outside while being inside. I could hear the winds and the birds. For three hours I barely moved from writing, immersed in memories of my relationship with my daughter Talia, who just left home for college. Yet all the while the grounds of Anam Cara were calling.

I finally closed my computer and headed outside, down a wet path by the side of the house and down mossy stone steps. The sound of rushing water filled my ears. An astonishing plant was growing beside the stairs, with leaves bigger than any I have ever seen in my life. The leaves had a shape similar to Lady's Mantle, but a single leaf was literally five feet wide. It was something you would have likely encountered in the Amazon rainforest. I never imagined finding something like that in Ireland. It was so outside of the average expectable, so gigantic, that it felt like it simply could not be true, yet there it was. Maybe like meeting a dinosaur, not part of the scale of the ordinary.

I continued to descend the stone stairs and came to a spectacular waterfall. The air felt charged—the place was pulsing with aliveness. It brought to mind another much smaller, but beloved waterfall in Western Massachusetts that I would regularly visit 25 years ago, when I was living alone in the woods after my first divorce. Relaxation and peace filled me. I heard the rushing of water, felt the moisture on my skin, watched the eddies foam as they cascaded over the rocks. All of this had been waiting for me below, as I sat in front of my computer screen, engaged with memory, of my complicated beloved girl who will never be under my roof again in the same way. And yet this opens the door to all sorts of new adventures and wonders, like this astonishing rainforest with its mythic foliage and magical waterfalls.

–Judy Tsafrir

Island Song

I am drawn to island life, and Ireland does not disappoint. It's a good place to awaken from paralysis, deadening and fear. Surrounded by her waters, I feel held, protected and still. On this island, I can hear the ancient song; it's time to return to my inner sea.

As a young woman, I dove deep in and swam with the invisibles. And then I got kicked in the ass by life. I felt ashamed and exposed. I was drowning. With great determination, I got out of the water and ran. As a land dweller, the veil closed. It was a surprising relief, even pleasurable. I was less irritable and I had more company. But I disappeared.

I'm aging, I miss myself and I miss the invisibles. Ireland sings, "Come, explore the mysteries, plunge head first into the turbulence and ride the waves." Fear grips me and I remind myself that in time I will wash up on to the shore, with a message in a bottle, a mysterious song, my inner sea.

–Suzanne Daub

Bridhe's Well

Today I am brought to the Saint's well
And I become the well.
I am thrown underwater
To count the joys and sorrows –
Spoken and unspoken
That were put into her care.

My heart rips wide open
Overflowing with the water of life.
Life made fluid
Flowing from person to person.

I see us become one –
Each unique and yet
United in the ancient Goddess.

–Ursi Barshi

Mother Well

The misty fog has swallowed them whole. They disappeared in an instant, those hardy and brave writers who I have come to love so deeply. Their suitcases lined the hallway like standing stones, giving mute testimony and reality to their impending departure. One by one, they hugged their goodbyes. They were on their way to board the bus and get to the airport on time. I have stayed behind in Kildare two more days to contemplate, absorb, and write.

The quiet feels strange. It is early morning, and I return to my room and snuggle deeply back into bed. The dark curtain stays closed to the dim light. It is Sunday, and it is quiet.

The happenings of the last two weeks are truly mind boggling. Sacred place after sacred place became a moving collage in my mind, a waving energy that carried me along like the weather, sometimes gently rolling, and at other times tossing me on a rough sea as I tried to understand what was happening. My cells are being rearranged. My consciousness is being stretched to accommodate so much new information.

Is it time to return to Brigid's well? I did, just then, return in my mind.

I like better the older, original well. It is still water, so clear, so quiet. Leaves float on the surface and reflections capture the overhanging tree branches above. The water itself seems lost in time. Present moment lingers, unable to move forward. I witness myself in the presence of this stillness. We each had dipped our bottles into its coolness to capture and carry home the liquid fluid memories of our time here.

Yes, I will physically return soon to the well to tie my offering to the tree branch there. Two turquoise beads strung together. One for me, one for my mom. They will remain there, suspended above the sacred well, joining us together in love and healing. This intention is already reaching my mother through the invisible airwaves that link us. She is happy, as am I.

But still, I do not yet walk.

I am in bed, suddenly sleepy beyond measure. I cover myself with the comforter and fall asleep hugging myself, the triple spiral necklace dropping softly from my neck as I curl into a fetal ball inside my own womb.

I awake two hours later to the sounds of merry maids in the hallway. They are making tidy the rooms of the departed ones.

Wait. There was a dream. An image sits in my mind. It was of a tiny figure, not human, but like human. He had large pointy ears and pointy shoes and a brown pointy hat sitting on what possibly was a pointy head underneath! His hands and feet were resting on a stone rectangular frame and his body was suspended above a small pool of water which he was gradually sinking into, face forward. Then, his whole body touched and submerged below the surface. I was falling into the well along with him, then suddenly, I am him. I let myself sink sink sink, fall fall fall into the clearness, the clean waters of the well. The surrounding blackness does not frighten me.

The chatter in the hallway brings me back again. Soul cracking open. Love brought me here. Love of and for the Divine. Adventure of the spirit—to be loved and nourished and returned to the Divine, healed and whole, no questions asked, no questions needed, no answers expected or desired.

It is now 1:00 pm and I am still hidden in the monastic cell of my room. I have yet to walk to the well.

I suddenly see the spirit of Brigid in my 2½-year-old granddaughter, Amu. Her fierce determination, unafraid, zooming forth into life. How do I give her my best as she grows more and more into herself? I think we will be growing together. I have long known that Amu will be my teacher, beginning with where my daughter left off. All those years ago, when my baby daughter was my only dancing partner as a single mom. How were we to integrate ourselves into life when we were orphans in the huge world, bereft of faraway family and living on welfare? When I wrote my parents that I was pregnant by a dashing and charismatic wandering minstrel who had already abandoned me, the news put my mother in bed for three days. She never took well to the idea of babies being born. Trouble. Indeed.

A crowd of crows beacon as I sit in a café. It is 3:30. I shall at last walk to the well.

I walk, my writing journal pressed across my breast, cherished as a Bible might be to a Christian. But this is my sacred book, my holy scripture, my sacred text, my truths, my story.

I walk. I walk to bring to home my sacred earthly mother. For without healing her, there is no healing of myself. The sky is so blue. The clouds so puffy, so fast flowing. Gone is the earlier cloud of mist. It is clear. I pass St. Brigid's Parish Church. Thinking to go inside, a young man and I arrive at the door at the same moment. It is locked. We shrug and go our separate ways. A family emerges from a car at the outskirts of town and the mother helps the girl put on a coat and her roller skates.

Past the Solas Bhride Centre. It is empty today as Sister Phil has gone to visit her 94-year-old mother, as she told me yesterday she would. "Ask her questions," I had said. What? I was giving advice to an ordained sister, one who has devoted her life to the care of others, and it shows so joyfully in her being. But out that popped, no less. How I long to be able to ask my mother questions. Many questions remain inside my heart.

Tell me more of your childhood, dear Mother. I want to know. I do know you were the Cinderella in the kitchen of your childhood home, the floor scrubber, the pie maker, the wringer of chicken's necks, the milker of cows, the girl afraid of her brothers, of that gleam in their eyes. Your older sister did what she could to protect you—all living out on the farm as you did. Your father was dead, and your mother never wanted your birth, as she told you on her deathbed. What kind of mother was she, my grandmother? The legacy of mothers. It isn't always grand.

This walk has become a pilgrimage, a journey home to my roots, to my mother. It is now to her that I walk. To help heal her pain. I have arrived. It is 4:30. The well. How simple. How old. The ancient memories gently bubble to the surface, as the well is fed from deep below, constantly cleansing itself from the sorrows of those who visit, transforming those sorrows into ones of healing. To heal. To be born anew.

I reach down to the water and baptize myself. I dip the turquoise beads, too, and ask "Okay, Mom. Are you ready?" I arise from the stones and tie the bead amulet to a small overhanging branch. I finish my incantations. I am at peace. It is 5:00 pm, and I am writing on the very last available clear page in my journal. It is time to go home.

I gaze one more time at the waters. They tremble again their welcome, and their goodbye. It is done.

–Jessica Webb

"The Healing Well"
–Jessica Webb
Acrylic on canvas, 24" by 30", 2016

Blessing

Blessing

As we prepared to board the bus yesterday for Newgrange, Sarojani smudged me with sage, and Carolyn blessed me with water—making the ordinary moment sacred. My heart opened, just as it had on the autumnal equinox, when I witnessed the rising Sun on that wind-swept summit of Loughcrew, with the moon still bright in the sky. I want to remember that feeling of heaven and earth joining together in my heart.

It's been at least eleven or twelve years since I have been blessed. There is a Jewish tradition of blessing the children on Shabbat. My father always blessed me. I always blessed my children. Since he died in 2005, no one has blessed me. The blessing Carolyn gave me brought him to mind.

I love blessing and being blessed. A devotional Jew recites at least 100 blessings a day. There are blessings for every occasion. There are specific ones for eating certain foods, for washing your hands, for urinating and defecating, for seeing a person with a deformity or witnessing a natural disaster.

Blessing consciousness feels alive on our journey; the magic of the passage mounds, oriented to the heavens and the celestial timing, Heaven and Earth united. And the three spirals, life, death and rebirth, the cycles without end or beginning, or always ending and beginning again. I want to carry the presence of Mystery and Magic with me. I want to have my heart be open to receive the beauty and wonder, always remembering to make the ordinary sacred with blessing consciousness.

–Judy Tsafrir

On the Bus to Castletownbere

We're on the bus, barreling down the highway between Navan and Castletownbere. I'm telling Judy the story of my mysterious first two years, and the remarkable last seven years of my life. Suddenly there is turbulence; we pull over to find the tire of the towed luggage carrier shredded into rubber ribbons. Holy shit, I think, my "baggage" is just too damn heavy and, quite frankly, dangerous.

We wait on the side of the road for the repair, but we are women, so we have to go to the bathroom. We walk together along the side of the road and find a steep vine-covered staircase leading down to a clearing. When we return to the bus, the decision has been made to unhitch the luggage carrier and travel to a roadside convenience store where we can wait out the repair.

We get off the bus at an Esso station. Esso! I am flooded with delightful childhood travel memories, Tony the Tiger—Put a Tiger in your tank! Oh how I have missed you, Tony.

We enter the store, and cross over a time portal. Unlike the American toxic dumps that we call convenience stores, this clean bright place is a roadside shrine. We buy a fresh lunch from a gourmet deli. We sit, chat, and make friends with the staff. We buy lottery tickets and are collectively bummed that we are not instantly euros richer.

The luggage carrier-bus combo gets sorted out and we prepare for the next leg of the journey, purchasing chocolate, popcorn, and sweets. Of course, we have to pee one more time. Back outside, I am stunned to notice the name of the place, Re:Store. It takes my breath away. "Restore. I get it." I love this place. Refreshed, repaired, restored and ready to resume life's journey.

–*Suzanne Daub*

Wedding Party

Two angel girls run
between stone walls
more ancient than St. Peter
their long dresses
sweeping around them
like the swirling mists
of Loughcrew

They look to be
the only happy members
of the wedding party
scattered around the remains
of Melefont Abbey
disheveled crows
squawking with mouths closed

The bride tries in vain
to keep her lush chestnut hair
from veiling her face
the groom tries not
to look ill-at-ease
also in vain
the bridesmaids wrap their arms
about themselves in an effort
to ward off the damp wind
the mother tries to keep
her bonny hat from flying away
& the men—well, they are just men
standing around the way men do

No one had promised them
a sunny September day
at Melefont Abbey
Just as no one had promised us
a glorious day at Lough Crew
We make what we get
& we get what we get

It's taken me many lifetimes
to realize this lesson
to step into a moment
to breathe it in
to accept it
to know it

As our bus pulls away
I hope the best
for the young couple
I hope the knowledge
of their moment
will surprise them
and lift them
in its joyful hands

–Linda Serrato

Blue-Eyed, Carrot-Topped Boy

A father and his young blue-eyed, carrot-topped boy, shy faced at the rest stop. Nothing is here by accident. The lad forgets to latch the washroom door.

Seeing the green Vacant display on the door, I open it. A glimpse of the boy standing. A shout.

"Oh! Okay," I say, and stand back. A flush. The door opens.

"I'm sorry," the boy says, eyes downward, already learning the particular power of shame.

"No worries," I call out, and suddenly I stop him in the hallway, this eight or nine-year old boy whose father waits outside. I squat down, reach out, tilt his chin upward, look into his eyes so he can see mine, shining.

With my finger, I trace a heart on his shirt, and say, "Listen to your heart. Only good comes from the heart." I urge him to have a belief in the marvelous, in enchantment, in things unseen, for somehow they will shore you up when humans, who are only being their flawed selves, wound or disappoint.

I tell him how fear eats away at a soul, as it did mine for so many years. Fear of being a disappointment, of something going wrong, of not being good enough. *Those* are the misguided myths that limit a person, and turn her into a small version of herself.

The Irish poet W. B. Yeats said long ago, "The world is full of magic things, patiently waiting for our senses to grow sharper." I feel impatient, out of time.

I hug the boy hard and say, "Go! Be brave! Listen to your unique song that courses like rivers under the noisy chorus that is our world. It is worth singing."

In truth, I didn't squat down. I didn't step into his path, tilt up his chin and speak. His father waited. Perhaps he was the better teacher after all. I stepped aside, hoping the boy could read my mind. I sent these blessings silently from across the rest stop aisle, into the sweet air of his blue-eyed being.

-- Jennifer Comeau

Insomnia

It's 2:30 am, Ireland time. I have been awake almost two hours. Again. I need sleep to keep my balance, stay healthy and open to my companions and the land. Such an old adversary, this inability to sleep. At an early age, my electrical wiring was disrupted in ways I'm still repairing. Over the past two decades, with a lot of experimentation and help, I have figured out how to manage insomnia. During the last week, the time change, varying schedule, and stimulation of being in a new place with new people have reawakened it.

Usually I try not to wake Martha, my wife, in the middle of the night, but she is an ocean and a continent away; it's 6:30 pm, Seattle time. Deciding to spend a few of my precious 100 minutes of prepaid phone time, I dial her. She answers instantly, surprised and delighted. I tell the story she's heard several thousand times in our 39 years together. After that, a string of different ways to say "I love you." She describes a polarity treatment that's easy to do: lying on one side, place one hand on the opposite shoulder and the other on the opposite hip. Like hugging yourself. Like being hugged. We end the call. Twelve minutes.

Soon I fall asleep and wake to my alarm at 7:30 am. Martha is dreaming by then.

Our molecules are intertwined. My wife can calm me with her voice, transmitted through a small rectangular contraption I hold in my hand. Her voice changes the electrical currents running along my nerves.

What if the gap, the chasm, between me and that voice is not distance, but time? What if the voice belongs to the beloved dead, as well as the beloved living? What if people I could never have known in this body are literally in my body? What if my DNA is speaking to me in an ancient language? What if the microchimera—cells passed from mother to child, child to mother, during pregnancy and birth—what if they came down through the generations into my body and are singing?

My nerves strain to hear the song.

–June BlueSpruce

The Goose

I saw a goose the other day; she had a broken wing.
I took her home – no, not to stay, but quickly heal and fly.
I fed her, warmed her, set her bone and put on salve,
I told her of the wind –
which soon would carry her away.

She did not heal. I tried my best.
Her pretty wing still drooped.
The days grew shorter and I knew
She would not fly, not this year and not next.
She always waddled close to me and back into her nest.

A dark, long winter finally passed,
made way for Spring and greener grass.
I walked her in the garden and filled a pool for her.
She seemed content to swim and splash
but never tried to fly.
I flapped my arms to show her how,
I coaxed her and cajoled.
She honked, as if to laugh
and tell that she is meant to stay.

One early morning I went out
and heard her quack in a queer way.
A shiny object by her leg turned out to be a golden egg!
She nudged it in my direction like a gift.

I took it with a thank you and looked at it with awe.
I turned it in my hands and saw that it was cracked.

I pried it open –
and to my surprise there was a whoosh in it –
and voices

whispering stories in my ear.
They buzzed around my head
and fluttered as if they did have wings.
I watched confused, I listened long and hard.
And then I understood.
I knelt down in the grass, all touched.
I hugged that goose, I petted her and cried:
"My darling little goose!
Despite your crooked wing
You found a way to fly!"

This story is the first of many,
but not the last for sure!
The egg is holding more
than we can ever count.
With a keen ear
I want to catch these words on wings,
and tame them with my pen.
All the while
the goose will quack contentedly
and close her eyes
and take a magic nap.

–Ursi Barshi

Healing

At Mary Madison's place in Eyeries, waiting for my stone reading, I head outside in misty rain to explore her exquisitely decorated gardens. At every turn, beauty, whimsy, the energy of *aos sí*, the faerie folk. Doorways to the Other World. I wander past a pond with geese, clumps of heather, altars with saints and faeries, shells and stones. The pyramid house for prayer and meditation, next to a full-size rowboat with its papier-mâché crew, a fisherman and fisherwoman, their green net filled with scallop shells.

I enter the pyramid through a wooden door inlaid with stained glass depicting Moses in the bulrushes. Removing my shoes, I sit on a wicker chair with bright red cushions under a skylight. As soon as I close my eyes, I have a vision of Brigid: Celtic goddess of fire, tall with long golden hair, emanating light. She faces me, circles moonwise, healing me as she goes, then faces me again and bows. I bow in return. Then I see *An Cailleach*, Irish earth goddess, mountain crone of the West, dark and fierce. As she circles, she removes sharp shapes from my energy field. We bow to each other.

Then Mary Madison appears in my vision, a gifted, petite, lively, sharp-featured woman with a mist of white hair. But wait: she's doing a stone reading in her house for one of my traveling companions. How can she be here?

"Am I distracting you?" I ask.

"I can be in more than one place at a time," she assures me.

I feel a twinge of pain in the left side of my neck and shoulder. "Overuse," she says, coming to my right side. "The energy flow there is closed off and has been for a long time. So the left side overworks. You are very advanced in feeling and intuiting but not as strong in asserting and doing in the world."

"But I've done a lot in the world!" I protest.

"Yes, but that work was all focused in the mind," Mary responds. "Now it's time for that energy to spread throughout your body."

I see all three: Brigid, *An Cailleach*, Mary Madison. Again, we bow. Then a message: "It's time to go." I put on my boots, go outside, continue wandering.

Sitting at the round blue wooden table outside Mary's kitchen, overlooking the koi pool lined with hundreds of shells and tiny fantastical figures, the rock wall topped with heather and adorned with faeries sliding down its face, and beyond, the harbor, I feel welcomed, at home. I belong here.

–June BlueSpruce

At Mary Madison's, County Cork

Normally,
I have to put in earplugs
in order to hear the silence
in order to hear the faint
murmuring of my heart.

Normally,
my voice is buried
beneath the everyday:
grandbabies, the music
of Mike Love, the juggling
of pots and pans by my grown son.

These are not bad sounds, no,
and these have been the sounds
of my life for some months.
But, they are not my sounds
that fall the way a rose
petal falls to the ground.

My voice has not been
coming to me lately.
She's been hiding in shadow
or fluttering just beneath
the hummingbird's wings.
I've watched her from
my front window

dancing with the bees,
hopping from arm to arm
on the big sage.
Yet, I didn't call to her

always being distracted
by a spill or a hug
or grunts from my grandson.

It's taken a 3-hour car ride
a 10-hour flight and
some bus rides
for us to meet again.
The bird was a good scout;
she tracked me down
across a continent,
across an ocean,
across a lush green island.

She found me
so that I could hear
the pounding of my heart
on the way to Loughcrew,
songbirds trilling between rain showers.

the rush of the wind
bringing back a love,
the whispering footsteps
at Anam Cara.

Now I sit in Mary's kitchen
on a finger of land
that aches with memory,
gazing at the Atlantic
and a collection of stones
and shells on the windowsill.
Normally,
the air around me
is filled with a menagerie of noise,
but today,
today
I hear the fluttering
of a thousand hummingbirds
and a voice,
my voice
sailing through the wind.

–Linda Serrato

"Feather Carvings"
–Janis O'Driscoll,
Clay Print, 11.75 x 15", 2016

On Returning

The garden insists her seasons into my bones once again. Not just our backyard garden, which will be planted with narcissus and tulip bulbs when we return home, but other gardens, where bees live, make honey and hives, all the while doing their grand dances, season upon season, moon over moon, rain over rain, wind upon wind, drinking sweet nectar presented to them in any weather.

I see that life presents itself to me now. I do not know for how long, but that's ok.

Does a bee know how long it will live? Does a butterfly open her cocoon knowing how many days she has left?

Does the acorn seed fall to the ground and spend time in the dark wondering how long it will be until it sees the light of day? It trusts the elements where it's been planted. When the loamy soil encircles its possibility, one day or night moonshine will signal and say, "Come, now begin to rise. Send your stem up and lay your roots down." The acorn in its evolutionary wisdom will begin its slow push up and pull down to make itself into the oak tree. The humming continues along with all the wisdom of the ages.

I take the acorn into my hand. I bless its past, its now and its possibilities.

I take my own hands, one into the other, and bless my past, my now and my possibilities.

Let me be washed with rainwater. May clouds pour over me from head to toe as I begin to pull more into earth day by day. I know I am not done here in this form—freckled skin, gray hair, long legs, good brain, warm heart. I am now an oak with deep roots.

A group of oaks stand by my side. We stand together, facing each day. Breathing in the air of night, hoping to remember the wisdom given to us on day one.

–Jean Mahoney

The Gas Station

And then there was the corner gas station,
where we stopped for a wee break.
The station sign was Gaelic,
and everywhere we turned,
green fields, the scent of Ireland, and everything
had another life, another language.
As if we had stepped into a slight bend
in the story we tell ourselves,
we fourteen women standing outside
in line for the little stall. All around,
Irish voices floated in ancient song
blessing us and the grasses.
The corner station was lit somehow,
with a drench of the Otherworld,
except we were the Other—
they were Home. It was we who abided
in a strange, separate existence.
Inside, the tall man at the counter
gave directions in an ancient brogue.
But where we were headed,
he could only point the way.
It was up to us to find it.
The sun peaked gray
and silver through the clouds.

–Carolyn Brigit Flynn

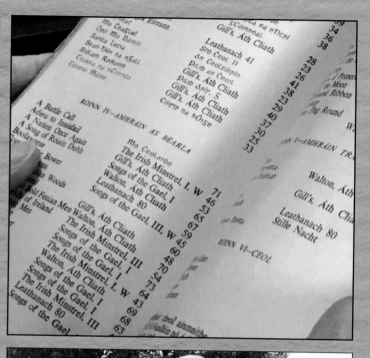

CONTRIBUTORS

CAROLYN BRIGIT FLYNN, Editor, is a writer, poet and teacher. She is the author of the poetry collection *Communion: In Praise of the Sacred Earth* and the editor of the anthology *Sisters Singing: Blessings, Prayers, Art, Songs, Poetry and Sacred Stories by Women*. Her memoir *The Light of Ordinary Days*, set against the backdrop of Irish history, mythology, geology and more, is forthcoming in 2020. Carolyn is a writing teacher in Santa Cruz, CA, and periodically brings groups of writers and artists to Ireland for writing retreats and tours. carolynbrigitflynn.com

JANIS O'DRISCOLL, Designer, is an artist, photographer and printmaker who translates pencil, marker, and ink drawings into intaglio and relief prints. She is a member of the Printmakers at the Tannery Cooperative in Santa Cruz, Ca, and serves on its board. She has exhibited her work in juried shows in California and New York state, and frequently in the Santa Cruz and Monterey Bay area. As a professional librarian, Janis has spent her life steeped in literature and writing. The 2016 journey to Ireland was her first visit to the home of her ancestors. http://pattpress.org/janis-odriscoll/

URSI BARSHI is an artist and writer born in central Switzerland, where she grew up with fairy tales and local folklore. As a painter and textile artist, she creates puppets, figures, sculptures and felted paintings. As a kindergarten teacher she developed stories, plays, songs and puppets to design curriculum on essential skills. Ursi was drawn to Ireland by its rich mythology, art and deep connection to the land, which reminded her of the alpine landscape of her homeland. She lives in Santa Cruz, CA.

JUNE BLUESPRUCE is a writer, activist, life coach and shamanic practitioner. Her poems have been published in *off our backs, Northwest Passage, South Seattle Emerald, Sisters Singing: Blessings, Prayers, Art, Songs, Poetry and Sacred Stories by Women, My Lover is a Woman: Contemporary Lesbian Love Poems,* and *I Am Ready to Speak.* She is the author of the poetry chapbook *clear cut.* Her blog on dreaming, healing and activism is at www.junebluespruce.com/blog. June worked for many years in health care delivery and research. She now works with community-based groups on tree protection, climate change, women's and LGBTQI rights, and social justice. She lives in Seattle, WA.

116

JENNIFER COMEAU is a writer, singer-songwriter, and engineer who inspires humans to remember and restore our sacred partnership with the natural world. A finalist in the 2014 Maine Songwriting Competition, her two music CDs "She Flies" and "Feed the Tribe" are available online (iTunes, YouTube, CD Baby). Jennifer has recently completed *A Moon in All Things*, a novel-with-songs set in 1820's Ireland. Her retreat workshops take place at Sanctuary at Sunrise Hill, located in Kennebunkport, Maine. www.jennifercomeau.com

SUZANNE DAUB is a mosaic artist and photographer who turns to art as a meditation. She is on the Board of Directors of the Mosaic Society of Philadelphia and shows her work in local galleries. Her artwork involves working with tile, glass and stone, and she was thrilled to encounter the carved megalithic stones of Ireland in 2016. As a clinical social worker, Suzanne focuses on improving the health and wellness of poor and vulnerable populations, and is a national leader on this topic. She has won the Innovations Award from the Pennsylvania Association of Community Health Centers. She lives in Philadelphia, PA

SANDY DEMPSEY spent 35 years as a social worker/activist devoted to the prevention of and healing from interpersonal and family violence. She served as Legal Director for Women Organized Against Rape, Executive Director of Philadelphia Physicians for Social Responsibility, and Co-Director of the Institute for Safe Families. She joined the Ireland writing retreat to reconnect and make peace with her father in his ancestral homeland. While there, she fell deeply in love with cows and has become an advocate for ethical dairy farming. She devotes her creative life to writing and mosaic art. She lives in Philadelphia, PA.

ANNE FITZGERALD is a writer, international activist, and founder of the consultancy ~Spirit at Work Globally~. An executive leadership coach and facilitator, she has organized women's leadership and empowerment projects. Her current focus is honoring indigenous wisdom and the earth. In 2008, she brought BEADS 4 PEACE to the US, to enable AIDS widows from Meru, Kenya to sell their beaded jewelry. Anne serves on the Board of International Peace Initiatives and the leadership council of Women of Spirit and Faith. She was a facilitator at the Parliament of World Religions in Spain and Australia. Having previously traveled to Ireland to meet her Irish relatives, she was thrilled to return in 2016. She lives in Waltham, MA.

NORA JAMIESON is a writer and psychotherapist, and the author of *Deranged*, a book of three short stories which was a finalist for the Indie Book Award in 2016. Her work has appeared in *Dark Matter: Women Witnessing* and *Sisters Singing,* and she publishes occasional essays on her blog at www.norajamieson.com. Nora established Women's Temple, Earthspirit Council House. After many years of writing about the dead, Nora is now an apprentice to grief, mourning her beloved husband of 37 years, Allan Johnson. She lives in Canton, CT.

JEAN MAHONEY is a writer, poet and award-winning educator whose writing has appeared in the *Santa Cruz Sentinel* and *Sisters Singing: Blessings, Prayers, Art, Songs, Poetry and Sacred Stories by Women.* She is the author of *Brave Hearts: A San Francisco Story: The Grit and Dreams of an Irish Immigrant Family,* which tells the tale of four generations of her family in America. She taught sixth grade in public school in Santa Cruz for twenty years, and worked as a pioneer in environmental education and the movement for Life Lab school gardens. She later helped to design and present teacher training programs in the California Environmental Education Initiative curriculum. She lives in Santa Cruz, California.

SAROJANI ROHAN is a writer, musician and educator who first traveled to Ireland in 2004, where she discovered her love of Irish music. Upon returning, she established the Celtic music group, Innisfree. She has since returned to Ireland four times for inspiration and renewal. Her poems have been published in *Monterey Bay Poetry Review, Landscape of Poetry and Soul,* and *Sisters Singing.* She has published articles on education and working with young children based upon her 38 years as a teacher. She lives in the mountains of Santa Cruz, CA.

LINDA SERRATO is a retired teacher and poet whose work has been published in *Along These Lines, Travelogue for Two: Poems by Sanford and Friends, re:home photographers and writers, Sisters Singing,* and *Watershed Literary Magazine.* As a young poet, she was awarded the Josephine Miles Award by the American Academy of Poets. In 2013, she won the Editor's Poetry Prize from *Floodplain Literary Magazine.* Linda helped to organize public school teachers, and is involved with workers' rights and human rights. She received her MA in Creative Writing from San Francisco State University, and lives in Chico, CA.

JUDY TSAFRIR is a Board Certified holistic adult and child psychiatrist and psychoanalyst on the faculty of Harvard Medical School. She has a private practice of holistic psychiatry with a special interest in Environmentally Acquired Illness in Newton Center, Massachusetts. She is also a professional astrologer, tarot reader, shamanic practitioner, painter and writer. Her paintings have been included in exhibitions at The Boston Psychoanalytic Society. She writes about medicine and healing in two blogs, "Adventures in Holistic Psychiatry" at www.JudyTsafrirMD.com and "Holistic Psychiatry" at Psychology Today.

JESSICA WEBB is an artist whose works are evocative renditions of the world and the sacred. Her paintings have been shown at the William Park Studio in Portland, OR, Townshend's Tea Gallery in Eugene, OR, and Anavami Studio in Santa Cruz, CA. She is a longtime meditator and practitioner of Surat Shabd Yoga. She has also studied with Martin Prechtel, a noted indigenous wisdom teacher. She lives in Portland, OR.

GERARD CLARKE, author of the Foreword, is an ecologist and history/archaeology guide. He has worked at Newgrange and was Head Guide at the Hill of Tara for five years. He works as the Outreach Officer for the Columban Missionaries in Dalgan Park, Navan. His specialty is Education and Ecology. He works with students and local communities to promote awareness and care for the earth and to develop a tree culture in Ireland. Born in Mayo, he has worked in Europe and North America and briefly in Asia. He now lives in Meath, Ireland.

PHOTOGRAPH ATTRIBUTIONS AND LOCATIONS

p. 6: BlueSpruce, Dzogchen Beara Buddhist Meditation Centre, Allihies, Beara Peninsula

p. 9: BlueSpruce, Dunboy Castle, Castletownbere, Beara Peninsula

p. 10: *(top)* Daub, Kildare; *bottom right)* O'Driscoll, Healy Pass, Beara Peninsula; *(bottom left)* Rohan, Castletownbere, Beara Peninsula

p. 12: Tsafrir, Healy Pass, Beara Peninsula

p. 14: *(top left)* Flynn, Eyeries, Beara Peninsula; *(top right)* O'Driscoll, Beara Peninsula; *(bottom right)* O'Driscoll, Ardgroom Stone Circle, Beara Peninsula; *(bottom left)* Comeau, Beara Peninsula

p. 20: *(left)* Serrato, Dunboy Castle, Castletownbere, Beara Peninsula; *(top right)* Barshi, Eyeries, Beara Peninsula; *(bottom right)* Tsafrir, Kildare

p. 22: O'Driscoll, Loughcrew, Boyne Valley

p. 26: Daub, Loughcrew, Boyne Valley

p. 27: O'Driscoll, Loughcrew, Boyne Valley

p. 28-29: *(left to right)* O'Driscoll; Daub; O'Driscoll; O'Driscoll; all Loughcrew, Boyne Valley

p. 31: *(top left)* O'Driscoll; *(right)* Flynn; *(bottom left)* O'Driscoll; all Loughcrew, Boyne Valley

p. 32: O'Driscoll, Loughcrew, Boyne Valley

p. 34: O'Driscoll, Loughcrew, Boyne Valley

p. 37: Daub, Loughcrew, Boyne Valley

p. 38: Flynn, Newgrange, Boyne Valley

p. 40: Daub, Newgrange, Boyne Valley

p. 43: Rohan, Knowth, Boyne Valley

p. 44: Serrato, Bective Abbey, Boyne Valley

p. 45: *(top left)* Serrato, Rathmore Church, Athboy, Boyne Valley; *(top right)* Comeau, Ardgroom Stone Circle, Beara Peninsula; *(bottom)* BlueSpruce, Newgrange, Boyne Valley

p. 46: BlueSpruce, Eyeries, Beara Peninsula (portrait of Mary Madison)

p. 48: Flynn, Rathmore Church, Athboy, Boyne Valley

p. 50: Tsafrir, Rathmore Church, Athboy, Boyne Valley

p. 52: Rohan, Brigid's Well, Kildare

p. 55: *(left)* Daub, An Tobar Retreat Centre, Navan, Boyne Valley; *(right)* Dempsey, Kildare

p. 57: BlueSpruce, Bellinter House, Navan, Boyne Valley

p. 58: Daub, Knowth, Boyne Valley

p. 63: *(top)* BlueSpruce, Ardgroom Stone Circle, Beara Peninsula; *(bottom right)* Barshi, Ardgroom Stone Circle, Beara Peninsula; *(bottom left)* Barshi, Dunboy Castle, Castletownbere, Beara Peninsula

p. 65: *(left)* BlueSpruce, famine sign, Monasterboice, Boyne Valley; *(middle)* O'Driscoll, Beara Peninsula; *(right)* O'Driscoll, Kildare

p. 67: *(left)* BlueSpruce, Kildare; *(right)* Rohan, Kildare

p. 68-69: *(left to right)* Rohan; Flynn; O'Driscoll; *Solas Bhride* Centre, Kildare

p. 70: O'Driscoll, Wild Atlantic Way

p. 73: Daub, Castletownbere, Beara Peninsula

p. 75: Comeau, Castletownbere, Beara Peninsula

p. 76: Daub, Anam Cara, Eyeries, Beara Peninsula

p. 79: BlueSpruce, Beara Pennisula

p. 80: Dempsey, Brigid's Well, Kildare

p. 86: Mahoney, Brigid's Well, Kildare

p. 89: Comeau, Bellinter House, Navan, Boyne Valley

p. 91: *(left)* Rohan, Navan, Boyne Valley; (right) Rohan, Navan, Boyne Valley

p. 92: Flynn, Mellifont Abbey, Boyne Valley

p. 95: Comeau, Newgrange, Boyne Valley

p. 96: Flynn, Bellinter House, Boyne Valley

p. 101: BlueSpruce, Eyeries, Beara Peninsula

p. 104: O'Driscoll, Kildare

p. 106: Mahoney, Beara Peninsula

p. 108: *(left)* O'Driscoll, Bellinter House, Navan, Boyne Valley; *(top right)* Flynn, Boyne Valley; *(bottom right)* Flynn, Hill of Tara, Boyne Valley

p 109: Daub, Newgrange, Boyne Valley

p. 110: *(top left)* Flynn, Kildare; *(top right)* BlueSpruce, Hill of Tara, Boyne Valley; *(bottom right)* BlueSpruce, Knowth, Boyne Valley; *(bottom left)* Bellinter House staff, Navan, Boyne Valley

p. 111: *(top left)* O'Driscoll, Newgrange, Boyne Valley; *(top middle)* Daub, Eyeries, Beara Peninsula (Mary Madison); *(top right)* O'Driscoll, Bellinter House, Navan, Boyne Valley; *(bottom right)* Rohan, Boyne Valley; *(bottom left)* Daub, Ardgroom Stone Circle, Beara Peninsula

p. 112: Flynn, River Boyne, *Brú na Bóinne* Visitor's Centre, Boyne Valley

p. 113: *(top left)* Flynn, Rathmore Church, Athboy, Boyne Valley; *(top middle)* O'Driscoll, Beara Peninsula; *(top right)* Daub, St. Brigid's Well, Kildare; *(middle)* O'Driscoll, sketch, bridge at St. Brigid's Well, Kildare; *(bottom right)* Flynn, Loughcrew, Boyne Valley; *(bottom left)* Flynn, Bere Island, Beara Peninsula

p. 114-115: Comeau, Bective Abbey, Boyne Valley

122